MW00987862

The M16A1 Rifle

OPERATION AND PREVENTIVE MAINTENANCE

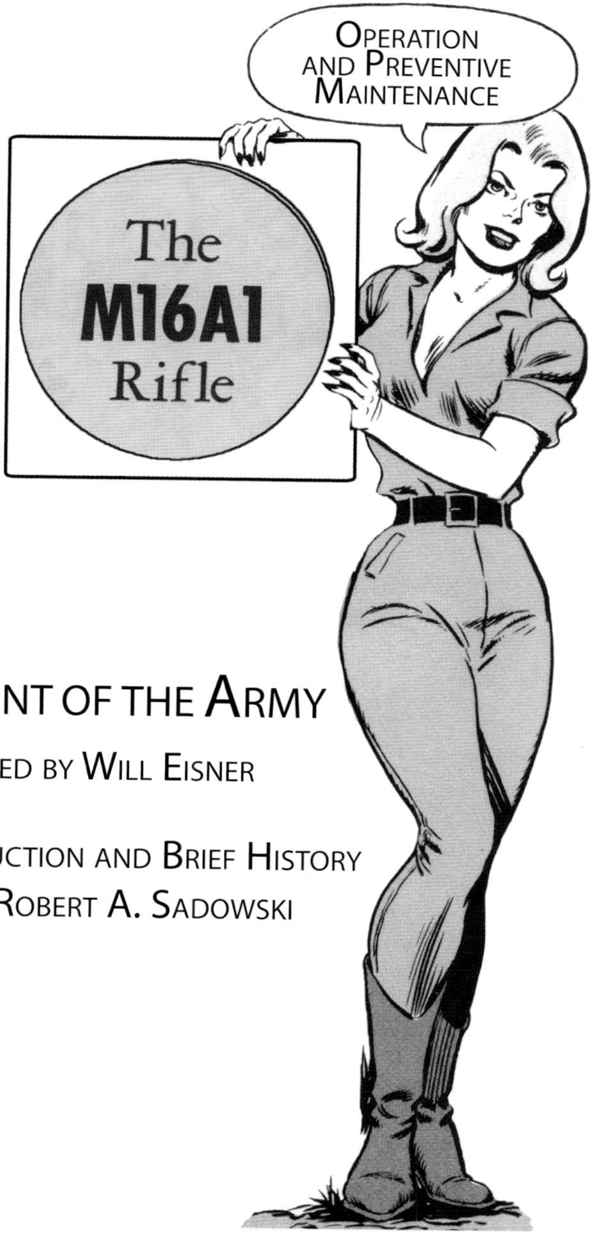
Operation and Preventive Maintenance
The M16A1 Rifle

Department of the Army

Illustrated by Will Eisner

Introduction and Brief History
by Robert A. Sadowski

Copyright © 2013 by Skyhorse Publishing
Additional material copyright © 2013 by Robert A. Sadowski

No claim is made to material contained in this work that is derived from government documents. Nevertheless, Skyhorse Publishing claims copyright in all additional content, including, but not limited to, compilation copyright and the copyright in and to any additional material, elements, design, or layout of whatever kind included herein.

Neither the author nor the publisher is responsible for damage to your firearm should you attempt to follow the disassembly/assembly and cleaning instructions contained herein. These procedures are presented as historical memorabilia and do not supersede manufacturers' recommended instructions and procedures.

All Rights Reserved. No part of this book may be reproduced in any manner without the express written consent of the publisher, except in the case of brief excerpts in critical reviews or articles. All inquiries should be addressed to Skyhorse Publishing, 307 West 36th Street, 11th Floor, New York, NY 10018.

Skyhorse Publishing books may be purchased in bulk at special discounts for sales promotion, corporate gifts, fund-raising, or educational purposes. Special editions can also be created to specifications. For details, contact the Special Sales Department, Skyhorse Publishing, 307 West 36th Street, 11th Floor, New York, NY 10018 or info@skyhorsepublishing.com.

Skyhorse® and Skyhorse Publishing® are registered trademarks of Skyhorse Publishing, Inc.®, a Delaware corporation.

Visit our website at www.skyhorsepublishing.com.

10 9 8 7 6 5 4

Library of Congress Cataloging-in-Publication Data

United States. Department of the Army.
  The M16A1 rifle : operation and preventive maintenance / Department of the Army; Illustrated by Will Eisner.
     pages cm
  Includes bibliographical references and index.
  ISBN 978-1-61608-864-4 (hbk. : alk. paper)
  1. M-16 rifle. 2. AR-15 rifle. 3. United States. Army–Handbooks, manuals, etc. 4. M-16 rifle–Pictorial works. 5. AR-15 rifle–Pictorial works. I. Eisner, Will, illustrator. II. Title.
  UD395.M2U53 2013
  623.4'425–dc23
                                   2013013212
ISBN: 978-1-61608-864-4

Printed in China

Table of Contents

INTRODUCTION

By Robert A. Sadowski

Have you ever read that booklet for your smart phone? Nope. How about your tablet device or computer? The manual for your vehicle? Not me. As loath as we are today to crack open a tome of dry, technical jargon it was same with G.I.s back in WWII. When Will Eisner was drafted into the U.S. Army in the early 1940s, the military had never heard of Joe Dope, but this comic character developed by Eisner helped train G.I.s to do their jobs better. Eisner used comics to educate by speaking to G.I.s in their own language. *PS, The Preventive Maintenance Monthly* instructed G.I.s on how to keep the jeeps, tanks, and other assorted pieces of equipment running, while also entertaining them. During the Vietnam War, when the newly issued M16 rifles started to jam at the precise moment they were needed in combat, the army brass enlisted Eisner's help to produce *The M16A1 Rifle: Operation and Preventative Maintenance*. The female narrator of the manual appealed to many of the boys in Vietnam during the late 1960s. A little "cheesecake" never hurts. But Will Eisner is not only remembered as a comic book guy who helped grunts in the sweltering jungle heat keep their black rifles throwing lead down range. Eisner is known for much more.

Eisner was instrumental in promoting and developing the medium we know as comics. Many comic book writers and illustrators owe a debt of gratitude to Eisner's strip, *The Spirit*, which was first inked in June 1940. This masked crime fighter, wearing a blue business suit, red necktie, and fedora, dispensed justice to a litany of villains in Central City. Along the way, The Spirit fought an archenemy—The Octopus—and ignored the seductive advances of femme fatales like P'Gell and Silk Satin, all the while sharing his adventures with his trusted side kick, Ebony White.

Eisner also helped establish the graphic novel as a new genre, and he took it to the status of literature with *A Contract with God and Other Tenement Stories*. *Last Day in Vietnam* is a collection of six short stories about combat and being behind the lines from WWII to Korea and Vietnam. It won the 2001 Harvey Award for "Best Graphic Album of Original Work." Though Will left us in 2005 at the age of 87, he is still paid tribute. "The Eisners," or more properly, The Will Eisner Comic Industry Awards, are given in recognition to certain individuals for their work and achievements in the comics medium.

The **M16A1** Rifle

OPERATION AND PREVENTIVE MAINTENANCE

Pam 750-30 1 July 1969
ersedes DA Pam 750-30, 28 June 1968)

The M16A1 Rifle
OPERATION AND PREVENTIVE MAINTENANCE

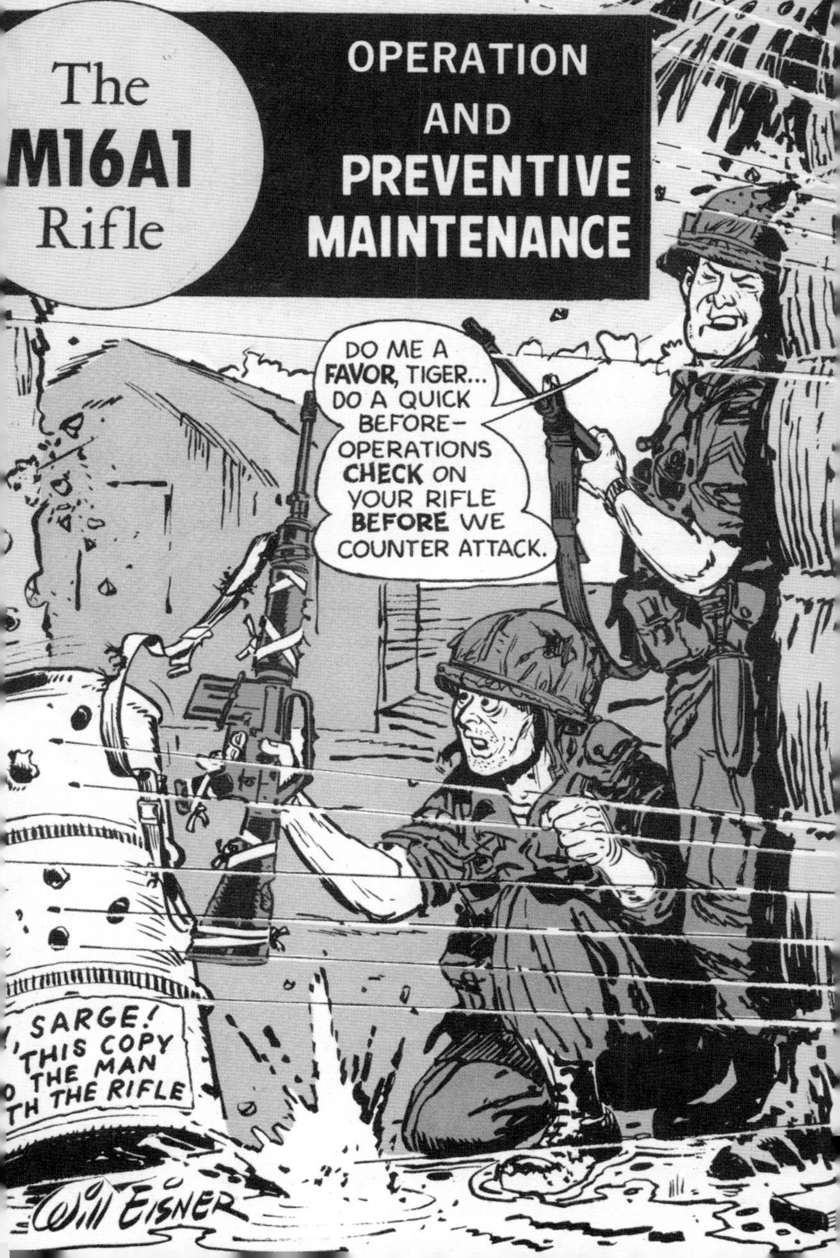
DO ME A FAVOR, TIGER... DO A QUICK BEFORE-OPERATIONS CHECK ON YOUR RIFLE BEFORE WE COUNTER ATTACK.
SARGE! THIS COPY THE MAN TH THE RIFLE
Will Eisner

You want to know her inside out, every contour and curve, every need and whim, what makes her tick.

No better time to get all-over acquainted than when you disassemble/assemble her for servicing.

Take it easy, no force . . . you could damage your chances in a showdown.

Eye-check the parts as you handle 'em. Get to know 'em by name and make sure they're OK for action.

Lay the parts down on a clean tarp or something in left-to-right order so that you won't lose any. Know how far you can strip, and stop right there.

OK, by the numbers now, start stripping— but gently. The orange numbers are for taking it apart; the black for putting it together.

TO KNOW ALL ABOUT YOU . . ."

HO

ST

YOUR B

COMES A FIREFIGHT— YOUR M16A1 RIFLE'S YOUR DEAREST NEXT O'SKIN—BAR NONE!

	DISASSEMBLY		ASSEMBLY	
1	Remove magazine.		Insert and seat.	16
2	Open bolt, check chamber for ammo.			
3	Press takedown pin to right with cartridge or finger.		Be sure selector lever's on SAFE or SEMI-AUTO before closing upper and lower receivers.	15
4	Pull back on charging handle and bolt carrier assembly.		Shove 'em in in reverse order.	14

DISASSEMBLY		ASSEMBLY
5 Take out the bolt and carrier assembly.		Put 'em back the same way, but be sure the bolt's unlocked. **13**
6 Remove the charging handle.		Hook the handle in, then shove it in. **12**
7 Push out the firing pin retaining pin.		Insert firing pin retaining pin, like so: Put the firing pin forward. The retaining pin goes in back of the large shoulder of the firing pin. Turn the retaining pin as you install it. **11**
8 Put bolt in LOCK position. Heed this: Never open or close the split end of the retaining pin.		
9 Remove the firing pin.		Install firing pin by dropping it in the hole. **10**
10 Take out bolt cam pin, give it a ¼ (90 degree) turn.		After you install the cam pin, give it a ¼ (90 degree) turn. **9**
11 Pull the bolt out of the carrier assembly.		When you install the bolt, be sure you stagger the ring gaps to prevent gas leakage. **8**
12 Use the firing pin to push out the extractor pin.		Insert the extractor pin. **7**

DISASSEMBLY		ASSEMBLY
13 Remove extractor and spring assembly for cleaning only. Remember not to lose, damage or separate them.		If you goofed and separated the spring from the extractor, insert the large end of the spring in the extractor and seat it. **6**
14 Remove the sling.		Install the sling. **5**
15 Take handguards off by first pulling down on the slip ring.		Install by first putting handguards in place, then push up on slip ring. **4**
16 Use the firing pin to release the receiver pivot pin.		Engage the receiver pivot pin. **3**
17 Separate the upper and lower receivers.		Join the upper and lower receivers. **2**
18 Push the buffer assembly in about ¼ inch, press in on the buffer retainer, then release the guide.		
19 Take out the buffer assembly and spring.		Insert the spring and buffer assembly. **1**

AND THAT' AS FA AS YOU'R ALLOW TO G STO RIGH HER

4

WHAT TO DO IN A JAM

THINK COOL, BUT ACT FAST

If your M16A1 rifle refuses to pop off — or quits popping sudden-like — you've got a stoppage that needs immediate action.

Immediate Action: Instinctively doing the right thing to clear your weapon and get it firing again, soonest!

Here's a slow motion of the procedure you'd best make second nature:

Tap upward on the magazine to make sure it's seated right.

Now pull the charging handle all the way back and see if a whole cartridge or case comes out.

If a cartridge or case is ejected, release the charging handle to feed a new round.

Careful, though, never "ride" the charger—let it go on its own.

Now, again hit the forward assist to make sure the bolt's closed . . . and pull the trigger.

MAYBE YOU GOT BAD ROUND, ...IMPERIALIST!

If she won't fire, now look for the cause . . . a bad round, busted firing pin or hammer spring, or whatever. Table 3-3 in your -12 TM covers causes and cures.

TRY TM.

If no cartridge or case ejects, first look for a round in the chamber. If none's there, once more release the charging handle to feed a round. Next hit the forward assist and again pull the trigger.

If she still won't fire, do what your TM says on trouble-shooting.

However, if you do find a cartridge or case in the chamber, be sure you remove it before you try to reload and recycle your weapon.

Now, remember, get these steps down pat.

CUE

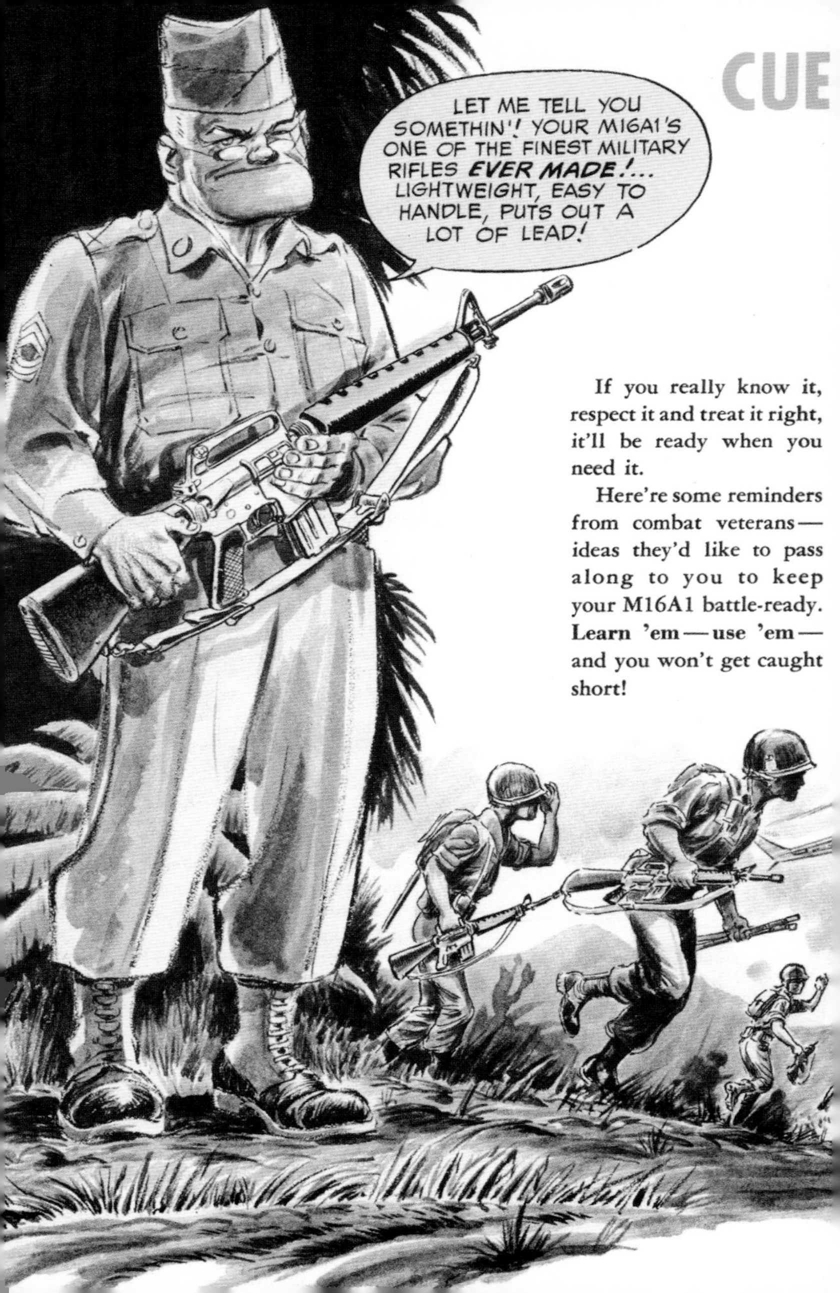
LET ME TELL YOU SOMETHIN'! YOUR M16A1'S ONE OF THE FINEST MILITARY RIFLES *EVER MADE!*... LIGHTWEIGHT, EASY TO HANDLE, PUTS OUT A LOT OF LEAD!

If you really know it, respect it and treat it right, it'll be ready when you need it.

Here're some reminders from combat veterans—ideas they'd like to pass along to you to keep your M16A1 battle-ready. **Learn 'em—use 'em—** and you won't get caught short!

OM GUYS WHO KNOW!

REMEMBER...
THE IMPORTANT THING
IS... *KEEP IT CLEAN!*

1 Keep your ammo and magazine as clean and dry as possible. The only part of the magazine that gets any lube is the spring — and it gets only a very light touch of LSA. Oil it up and you're headed for trouble.

CH LIGHTLY, PLEASE.

LSA

2 Inspect your ammo when you load the magazines. Never load dented or dirty ammo. Remember, **Never** load over 20 rounds.

3 Clean your rifle every chance you get — 3-5 times a day's not too often in some cases. Cleanliness is a must — and it may save your life!

AH, SWEET 16... AND YOU'VE NEVER MISSED!

4 Be sure to clean carbon and dirt from those barrel locking lugs. Pipe cleaners help here and inside the carrier key.

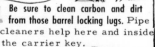

AND STAY OUT....

5 Never be bashful about asking for cleaning materials when you need 'em. They're available. **Get 'em and use' em!**

6 Check your extractor and spring often. If they're worn or burred, get new ones ASAP.

EXTRACTOR ————

———— SPRING

7 Lube your rifle, using LSA only. It's the most. A light coat put on with a rag after cleaning is good. Working parts need generous applications often. The chamber and bore need only a light coat after cleaning.

LSA

Worry a little more about your rifle . . . like, baby it a bit. F'rinstance, when you're out in the boonies, be careful where you put it down and how you put it down. Never drop it in mud or water or sand. Just keep in mind that you may have to use it before you get a chance to clean it.

TIPS THAT'LL KEEP
IT YOUR EVER-LOVIN...

SWEET 16

Here're a few cleaning and operating tips that'll help you get best results from your weapon. Some of these tips sort of put the accent on stuff you'll find in the rifle's bible—TM 9-1005-249-12 (1968) with Ch 1. Others are hexes and fixes direct from guys who've been living with this light-weight terro

TIP...

Here's something you want to be real careful about. Don't—like Never!—close the upper and lower receivers while the selector lever's in the AUTO position.

Always—like **Always**!—point the lever to SAFE or SEMI before closing the receivers.

Here's why: If you jam the receivers closed while the selector's in the AUTO position, you'll force the automatic sear down and damage the automatic sear, and the sear pin, and will likely rough up the bottom of the bolt carrier.

That's 'cause when the selector lever's in the AUTO position, the tang of the automatic sear moves to the rear. You can see how it works by opening the receiver and turning the selector to AUTO and watching the movement of the tang of the automatic sear.

So-o-o . . . do it right . . . every time. Point the arrow to SAFE. Then the receivers will close without any interference.

TIP...

Speaking of magazines . . . every guy has his own idea of how firm or loose he wants the holding action of the magazine catch to be. Which is A-OK as far as it goes. But remember this: The tighter the mag's held in the receiver, the more pressure it takes to release it. And this: The farther the shaft of the catch sticks through the catch button, the tighter the magazine's held in the receiver.

RELEASE MAGAZINE.

MAGAZINE CATCH BUTTON.

9

So, take a cue from experience. Adjust the catch button so's it's just about flush with the inner groove or just sticks out a tiny bit. This'll make the catch firm enough to prevent accidentally bumping the button and letting the magazine drop out—yet it won't be so tight that you can't pull the mag out for a quick re-load.

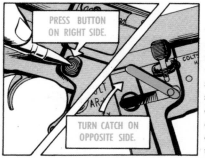

No sweat adjusting the catch the way you want it, either . . . and you're authorized to pull this deal. Just press the button on the right side of the rifle with the nose of a cartridge far enough so's you can turn the catch on the left side of the weapon. You turn the handle clockwise to tighten it and counterclockwise to loosen it. Best of all, you don't have to take the weapon apart to do this.

TIP . . .

You won't have any trouble with the new-type swabs listed in your new TM (FSN 1005-912-4248).

O'course, some guys've been complaining about old-type, big-size cleaning swabs jamming in the bore—and breaking the cleaning rod. You won't have this trouble if you cut 'em all into four equal squares before using 'em. Your bayonet will do the job if you don't happen to have a knife or a pair of scissors handy.

ALL THE WAY WITH NÉGLIGÉ

I TOLD YOU THAT RIFLE NÉGLIGÉ AIN'T A SUBSTITUTE FOR REGULAR PM.

Now that you've got a plastic coverall bag (FSN 1005-809-2190) to protect your M16A1 rifle against dust, sand, mud, water and such, here's how to use it in good health—yours and your weapon's.

First, make sure your rifle's cleaned and lubed **before** you bag it. This cover's an aid to PM, but it'll never replace the cleaning and lubing you'll always have to do regularly. In fact, with a rubber band closing—not to mention rips and tears—the bag's not guaranteed watertight, so-oo-o. . . .

Second, if you're gonna keep it bagged more than 24 hours, be sure you eyeball the weapon every day for signs of corrosion from any moisture or condensation that might form in the bag.

Putting it on—Stick the rifle in the cover, muzzle first. Then fold the cover end over the butt stock and slip the rubber band on.

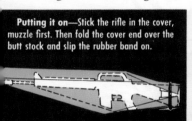

Taking it off—Slip the rubber band off and unfold the cover end. Then slide the rifle out.

Put it on and off gently and you can use the cover several times.

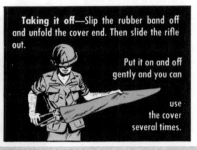

IN A FIREFIGHT

Comes a sudden opportunity to bag an enemy, here're 2 ways you can work it:

1. Quick-rip the bag off with one steady yank. The bag'll come apart at the tear-line.

2. If absolutely necessary, you can fire right through the bag. You can operate the selector lever and trigger easy with the bag on. But, remember this: Ejected cases will be trapped in the bag and could cause a malfunction after the first round. So get it off as quick as you can.

Natch, after "emergency" use, you'll need a new bag.

TOOLS FO
YOU

For Touch-Up Painting
(See Change 1
to your -12 TM)

Solid Film Lubricant...
12-oz spray can
FSN 9150-142-9309

Dichloromethane...
5-gal can
FSN 6810-244-0290

Here's a round-up
of the cleaning-
lubing equipment
you had better
use to keep your
M16A1 battle-
ready.
About the only
things different are
the M11E3 cleaning
rod and a PLASTIC
BOTTLE for holding
your LSA.
The big deal is to
use this equipment
every chance you
get.

- **Case, Maintenance Equi**
  FSN 1005-781-

- **Cleaning Rod** — Any one of
  these:
  M11E1 FSN 1005-903-1295
  M11E2 FSN 1005-999-2035
  M11E3 FSN 1005-089-3994

- **LSA**
  FSN 9150-935-6597

- **2 oz.**
  PLASTIC
  BOTTLE

- **Bore Brush** —
  FSN 1005-903-1296

12

Chamber Brush —
FSN 1005-999-1435

Pipe Cleaners —
FSN 9920-292-9946

Cleaning Swab —
FSN 1005-912-4248

Bore Cleaner
FSN 6850-224-6656

2 oz.
PLASTIC
BOTTLE

NEW CLEANING ROD

The M11E3 cleaning rod is a 5-piece affair (counting the swab holder as one piece), as compared to 4 pieces for the M11E1 and M11E2 Its over-all length is the same, though. Each section is shorter, that's all.

The threads on the E-3 are the same as on the E-1 and E-2, which means it takes the new bore and chamber brushes.

Don't sweat it, though. The new E-3's probably won't make the rounds till supplies of the E-1's and E-2's are gone.

BEWARE: DIFFERENT THREADS

Could be that some time you might have to use other cleaning tools in a pinch. If you do, here's what to look for: Different threads.

Your M16A1's own tools — cleaning rods and brushes alike — all have real fine threads . . . 36 to the inch.

But, if you're ever in a spot where you have to use any other rod, like the M11 (FSN 1005-070-7812) or any other bore brush like the one that carries FSN 7920-205-2401, or any other chamber brushes, like the M1 (FSN 1005-691-1381) or the M14 (FSN 1005-690-8441), watch this:

Their threads are coarser (32 to the inch). They won't match up with your authorized equipment. Don't try to screw 'em together. Won't work!

No sweat, though, on swabs. If you have the 30-cal type (FSN 1005-288-3565), just cut these big ones into 4 equal parts . . . and go ahead with your cleaning.

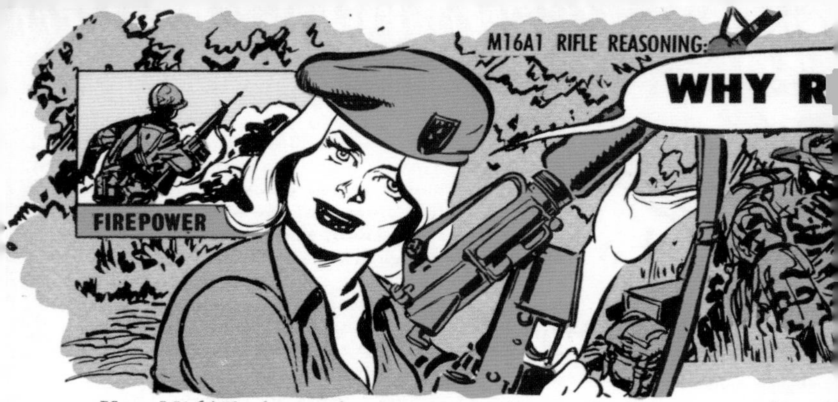

M16A1 RIFLE REASONING:
WHY R
FIREPOWER

Your M16A1's the spunky teenager of the small arms field, sure, but it's doing a man-size job. So it deserves reasonable treatment—especially in cleaning and lubing its lower receiver area.

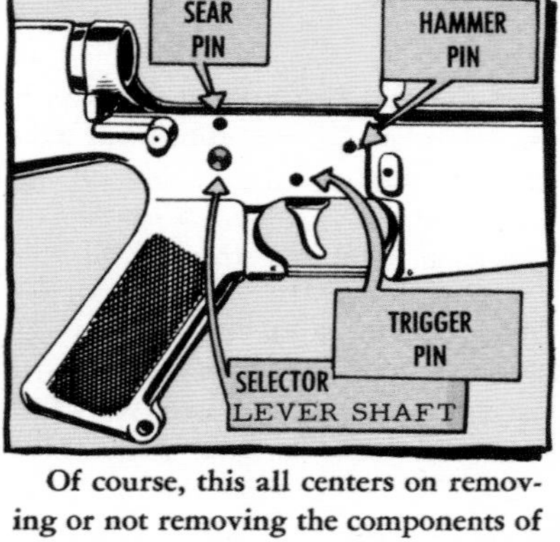

SEAR PIN
HAMMER PIN
TRIGGER PIN
SELECTOR LEVER SHAFT

Of course, this all centers on removing or not removing the components of the lower receiver to do the servicing job.

It's a fact. The 5.56-mm rifle doesn't like having its lower receiver taken apart for cleaning — and for good reason.

The lower receiver's made of aluminum to keep the weapon lightweight. But the pins that hold the automatic sear, the hammer assembly, th trigger and the selector lever are a made of steel.

So, if you keep taking the lowe receiver apart, these pins'll bye-n-by make the holes they go through bigge and bigger. First thing you know, th pins fall out and get lost — or th parts they hold won't line up right an your firing's 'way off.

Truth is, you are not authorized t remove the lower receiver's parts at all You can do a good cleaning job, if you do it this-a-way — and do it every day

1. Soak your artist brush (FSN 8020-244-0153) or other similar type brush real good with bore cleaner. Then scrub all the parts like there's no tomorrow to get off all the dirt and carbon you can.

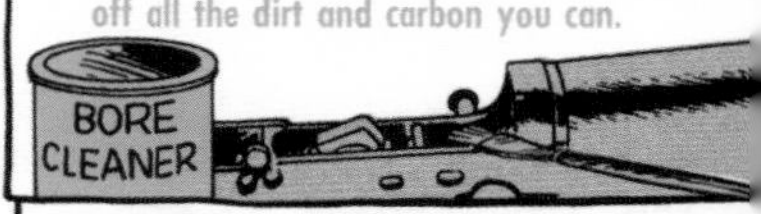

BORE CLEANER

2. Tip the lower receiver sideways to drain the excess bore cleaner from the cavity and then wipe it dry.

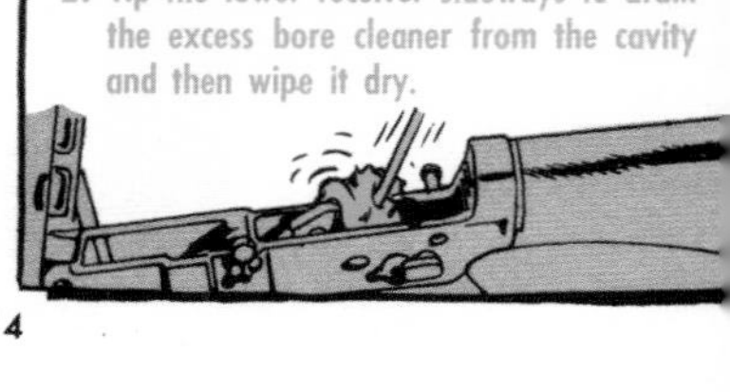

3. Wrap a piece of clean cloth or cleaning patch around the brush handle and poke it into the hard-to-get-at places. Do the best job you can to get rid of carbon and gook that could keep the parts from working right.

4. When you're all through — and the lower receiver's dry — put a generous coat of LSA (FSN 9150-935-6597) on all of the insides of the lower receiver and on all of the parts.

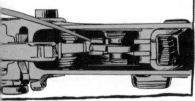

A cleaning job like this will get rid of all the carbon and dirt that might keep your weapon from shooting right. Any stuff that's left after you do your level best won't make no never-mind. Of course, if the lower receiver ever gets so fouled up that the rifle won't fire right, then you let support have a whack at it.

Now you can understand why TM 9-1005-249-12 (1968) with Ch 1, does not authorize disassembly of the lower receiver group for cleaning by riflemen and armorers. Parts replacement and extra-tough cleaning jobs are for direct or general support only.

But, please don't miss out on that lubing job. All components of the lower receiver — as well as the bolt carrier group — must wear a coat of LSA **at all times**. No "buts" about it. Your rifle can't perform without it.

That's why "white-glove inspections" are too risky for this baby. There's always the danger that some guy might be tempted to give his weapon a shower or tub bath before inspection to get rid of dirt and lube.

WELL, NO WHITE GLOVES TOMORROW, WE'RE INSPECTING M-16'S.

Anybody who bathes his rifle is doing it dirt two ways: First, he's robbing it of the lube protection it needs. Second, he's liable to let water seep into the lower receiver extension. This could cause corrosion of the extension and rusting of the action spring—or it might result in a short recoil of the bolt carrier group, thereby preventing the bolt assembly from retracting far enough to strip a cartridge from the magazine.

When you consider that all this has a direct bearing on how well your M16A1's going to fire and protect your hide in a showdown, these angles make real good sense, don't they?

MORE POINTERS TO PONDER

FOR YOU M16A1 **ZAPSTERS.!!** HERE ARE SOME NUMBAH ONE PM SUGGESTIONS TO KEEP YOU GO-GO!

HOW TO FIGHT CARBON FREEZE . . .

KEEPING A HEALTHY BOLT . . .

Another thing: When you're crawling or walking through the brush, make a mental note to make sure you don't get the flash suppressor caught in a bush. It catches easy, y'know.

All the way . . . Educate your sixth sense to flip the selector lever all the way across to get from Safe to Automatic. In an ambush situation, you just might flip it only halfway — to Semiautomatic — when you'll need all the fire you can get.

You might practice flipping it all the way till this becomes second nature.

All in all, this M16A1's a real sweet number. It'll stay that way as long as you treat it like one.

16

Combat types can't emphasize this enough: Clean the gas port in the bolt carrier group every day — and **take it real easy with the lube.** Dirt and powder-fouling — plus an overdose of lube oil — will give you a sluggish rifle. . . . Numbah 10 Thou' in a combat situation!

So, when you get your baby stripped for cleaning, like it says in para 3-9 in TM 9-1005-249-12 (1968) with Ch 1, take an extra 5 seconds to get at the port hole down there in the front end of the gas tube. Like so:

---

1. Work a worn bore brush full of bore cleaner around inside the key.

Make sure you get the metal end of the brush in all the way — right into the bottom of the hole where the gas tube is seated in the carrier key — and then turn it to loosen the crud. That last $\frac{1}{16}$-in there is the most neglected part on most M16A1 rifles.

---

2. Then use a pipe cleaner or the like to poke the gook out of the port. Don't use wire, though, or you might scratch the tube and set up worse trouble later on.

FSN 9920-292-9946
PIPE CLEANER

NOW IN YOUR TM

3. Use another pipe cleaner — or air-dry it by waving it around — to dry the tube as well as you can.

---

4. Now doublecheck your job. Remove the bolt. Then stick the carrier body into the receiver slideway and push the carrier back and forth **slowly** to check that the carrier key and gas tube line up OK. The carrier should move freely . . . and should go all the way without friction. If it won't go all the way without a struggle, you've got some more cleaning to do. But, if it binds, turn the weapon in for repair.

Here's the Pitch: The front end of the gas tube is self-cleaning, thanks to the hot gases and high pressure from the barrel. But, if you don't keep the other end clean — the gas tube area where it mates with the carrier key inside the receiver — brother! You've got to clean this area with elbow grease to prevent stoppages. Hear!

Now, when you come to lube-preserving, stick to the dope in the lube guide pages 22-24 of this pamphlet.

TIP...

HEY! CHECK FOR DIRT UNDER TH' EXTRACTOR.

THANKS!

Another couple places you won't want to forget when you're cleaning your weapon are the claw under the extractor in the bolt group and the locking lug recesses on the barrel extension in the upper receiver. If dirt and crud

CLEAN THE CLAW

USE NEW CHAMBER BRUSH ON LUGS

collect under the extractor, the claw won't be able to snap over the rim of a cartridge case. And if gook and brass chips from cases gather in the recesses, your bolt action will be stymied. So, bear down on your bore brush in both these places.

TIP... While you have the bolt group apart—and after you clean 'em—make a practice of eye-checking these parts:

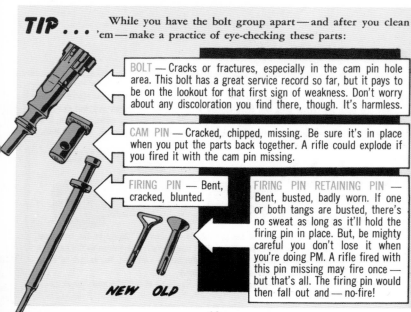

BOLT — Cracks or fractures, especially in the cam pin hole area. This bolt has a great service record so far, but it pays to be on the lookout for that first sign of weakness. Don't worry about any discoloration you find there, though. It's harmless.

CAM PIN — Cracked, chipped, missing. Be sure it's in place when you put the parts back together. A rifle could explode if you fired it with the cam pin missing.

FIRING PIN — Bent, cracked, blunted.

FIRING PIN RETAINING PIN — Bent, busted, badly worn. If one or both tangs are busted, there's no sweat as long as it'll hold the firing pin in place. But, be mighty careful you don't lose it when you're doing PM. A rifle fired with this pin missing may fire once — but that's all. The firing pin would then fall out and — no-fire!

NEW OLD

18

CLEAN ... INSPECT ... REPLACE

PARTS AS NEEDED

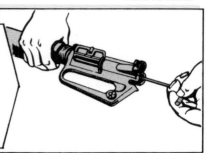

Chamber and Bolt Locking Recess: Clean 'em after every day's firing if you can. Use your chamber cleaning brush FSN 1005-999-1435 or any standard bore brush like the 30-, 45- or 50-cal or 7.62-mm brush. Dip the brush in bore cleaner ... get all the gook out of the chamber and bolt locking recess. Then dry the areas real good. Last, apply a light coat of LSA by wiping it with a swab dampened with the oil.

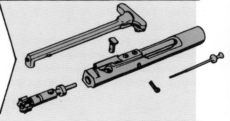

Bolt Carrier: Remove it from your weapon and field-strip it at least once a week. Use bore cleaner with any bore brush mentioned above and attack all parts, especially behind the rings and under the lip of the extractor. Clean the carrier key with your bore brush FSN 1005-903-1296 and bore cleaner. Then dry all the parts real good and coat 'em with LSA.

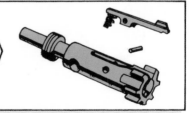

Extractor and Extractor Spring: Double check 'em every day, at least. Eyeball the extractor for chipped or broken edges in the area of the lip that engages the cartridge rim. Replace it if you find it damaged. Test the extractor spring by pressing on the extractor. If the spring's weak, replace it.

REMEMBER— Watch your lubing. Too much lube speeds carbon buildup in the chamber and bolt locking recess. Same thing with the carrier key. A rag or swab or even a pipe cleaner dampened with LSA will do the trick here. Best bet: Follow the guide on pages 22-24.

EVERY HIT COUNTS

Here're some coaching hints for a better season with your M16A1 rifle in the Vietnam League.

LAID A BUNT LATELY?

Probably not. But you could use the same idea when you're bore-brushing your weapon. Right. Choke up on the cleaning rod—hold it about 2 inches from the receiver and push it straight inch by inch in short jerks all the way through the flash suppressor. Then pull it back all the way out—again in short jerks. Never pull the brush back till after it's gone through the flash suppressor. Do it the right way and you won't hurt the rod.

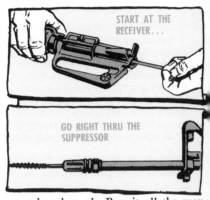

START AT THE RECEIVER...

GO RIGHT THRU THE SUPPRESSOR

Same idea goes when you're running patches through. Run it all the way through the flash suppressor before you start to pull back ... no matter what size patches you're using—the one for the M16A1 (FSN 1005-912-4248) or any large type that you have to cut into 4 equal squares.

DOUBLE-PLAY COMBINATION

OUT

OUT

GET HELP HERE !

By the way, when was the last time your unit armorer—Max Schnell, good 'ol Speedy Four—checked out your weapon? Don't know? Can't remember? Then it's due right now for a physical. Get with it! Maxie's the best partner you'll ever have ... PM-wise.

Here're a couple ways Maxie can shortstop trouble for you:

Any time you run into real trouble

with crud or carbon buildup when you're cleaning your rifle—especially in the bolt and locking recess area—get your armorer to help you tackle it with P-C-111 carbon removing compound, FSN 6850-965-2332, 5-gal pail

Some guys really spoil a play by reaching out for balls not meant for 'em. Bumped heads and lost games result.

Ditto for all parts of the upper receiver assembly. If any part gets bent — like the ears around the rear sight — or any part comes loose or busted, f'goshsakes, don't you try to fix it — nor you, either, Maxie! Turn the weapon in to DS.

And still one more: Natch, when you're field stripping your rifle you'll be careful not to drop the carrier and key assembly or bump 'em against anything hard. The carrier key bends pretty easy — and then won't line up inside the weapon. But, if they do get bent, don't you or your armorer try to straighten 'em. That's a drive too hot to handle. Let DS fix 'em.

You're bound to have a good season if you stay on the ball with your PM.

WATCH YOUR BUTT, TOO!

While we're gabbing about water, let's hammer home the importance of keeping it out of the lower receiver, too. This may not have anything directly to do with blowing up your shooter, but it could keep it from firing — which is the next worst thing.

Right, every time you clean your M16 — and every time you drain water from the bore — take an extra second to make sure the drain hole in the butt stock capscrew is open . . . and drain the butt, too.

A pipe cleaner's about the handiest thing for keeping this hole clear.

If water stays in the lower receiver,

CLEAR THE HOLE WITH A PIPE CLEANER

it'll foul up the working parts . . . cause corrosion and dampen your ammo.

So, remember, huh?

All of this boils down to one thing, then: Your **Prevention** is the **cure**.

Here're a couple-three lube tips that'll help you and your armorer get the most out of using LSA (Lube Oil, Semi-fluid, Automatic Weapons, MIL-L-46000A) on your 5.56-MM rifle — now that it's LSA all the way for the M16A1 zap-machine anywhere but in real cold-weather areas.

Yessir, LSA's here to stay. It does a better lubing job on working parts, especially in a muggy-wet climate like Vietnam's . . . it lasts longer . . . it really protects metal surfaces. Here're the stock numbers that'll fetch it for you: FSN 9150-935-6597—2-oz LSA tube; FSN 9150-889-3522—4-oz tube; FSN 9150-687 4241—1-qt can; FSN 9150-753-4686—1-gal can.

WHERE AND HOW MUCH LSA?

The big trick to using LSA is to get plenty of it on the working parts — like those inside the upper and lower receivers — and very light doses in other places — like the bore and chamber, inside the carrier key, inside the bolt and on the firing pin and the magazine spring — and none at all on your ammo or on the inside of your magazine.

CLEANING — Normally, you want your rifle spitting clean inside and out before you apply LSA. So do a real good job after every firing mission, following the good word in your TM by using rifle bore cleaner (CR).

Too busy fighting? OK, then postpone the cleaning BUT lube all the working parts with LSA **frequently** and **generously.**

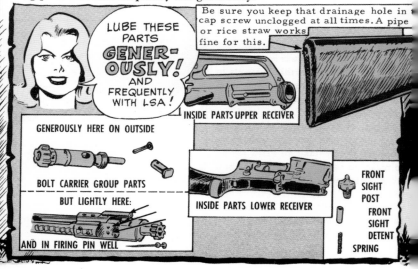

LUBE THESE PARTS **GENEROUSLY!** AND FREQUENTLY WITH LSA!

Be sure you keep that drainage hole in cap screw unclogged at all times. A pipe or rice straw works fine for this.

INSIDE PARTS UPPER RECEIVER

GENEROUSLY HERE ON OUTSIDE

BOLT CARRIER GROUP PARTS

BUT LIGHTLY HERE:

AND IN FIRING PIN WELL

INSIDE PARTS LOWER RECEIVER

FRONT SIGHT POST

FRONT SIGHT DETENT SPRING

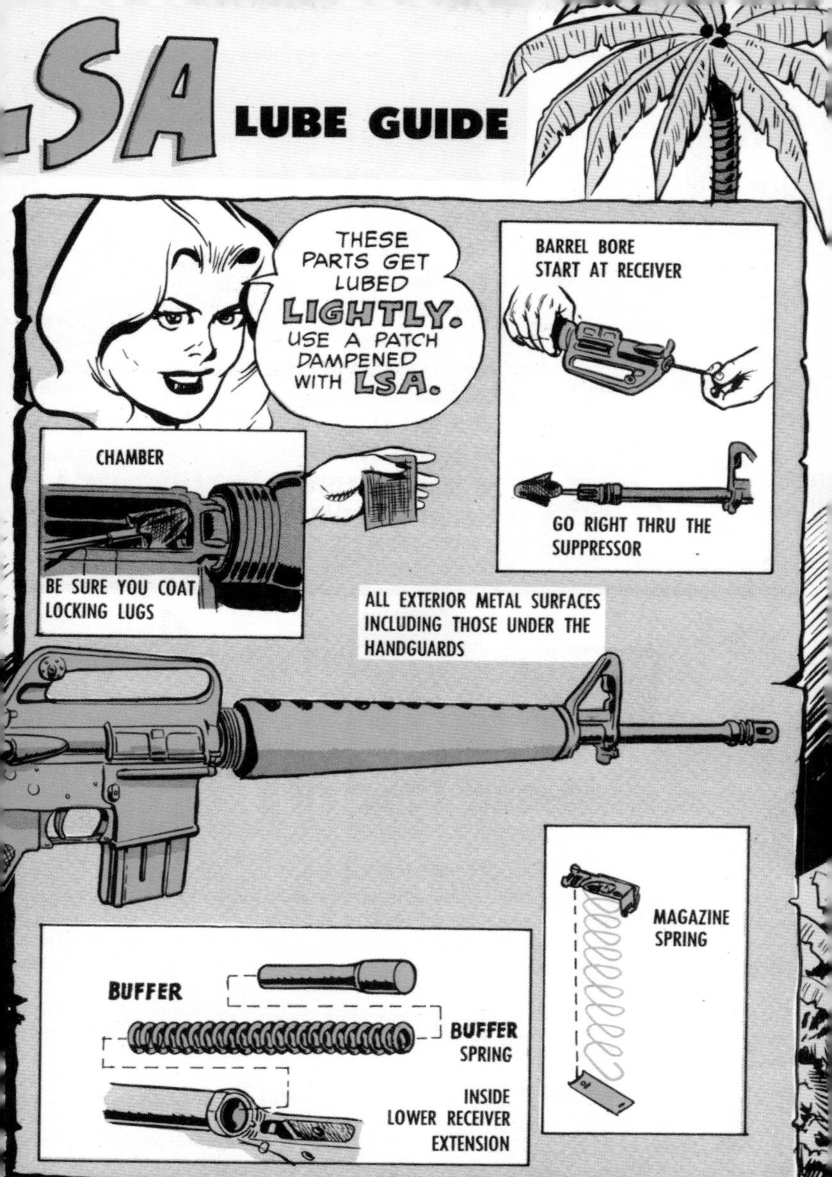
LSA LUBE GUIDE
THESE PARTS GET LUBED LIGHTLY. USE A PATCH DAMPENED WITH LSA.
BARREL BORE START AT RECEIVER
GO RIGHT THRU THE SUPPRESSOR
CHAMBER
BE SURE YOU COAT LOCKING LUGS
ALL EXTERIOR METAL SURFACES INCLUDING THOSE UNDER THE HANDGUARDS
MAGAZINE SPRING
BUFFER
BUFFER SPRING
INSIDE LOWER RECEIVER EXTENSION

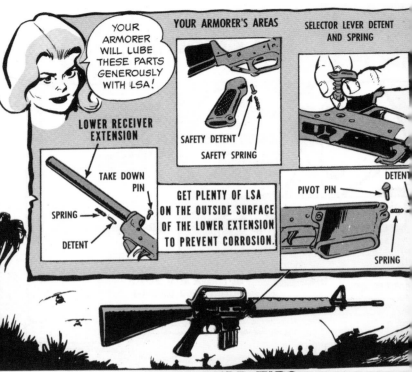

MORE LUBE TIPS

Say. . .having trouble with how much LSA it takes for a "GENERO
application?

Or what constitutes "LIGHTLY" lubricated?

Well, don't get excited. The terms are only general and are not
intended to designate a precise amount of lubrication.

Consider it generously lubed if the part is covered with enough LSA
that you can see an obvious film heavy enough you can wipe around with
your finger (you don't have to squirt her full).

If you have wiped on a coat of lubricant with a rag or swab moisten
with LSA, but it's still not so much you can really see a film on the pa
call it "LIGHTLY" lubed.

ZAPPER'S OWN M16 PUB

Hey, you M16A1 sharpshooters, be sure you latch on to TM 9-1005
249-12 (1968) with Ch 1. That's right -- "-12." It replaces all the oper
organizational dope in the -14 TM with all of its changes.

DRAIN BEFORE SHOOTING

THIS
CAP
WON'T
XCUSE
YOU
FROM
ILY (OR
FTENER)
ANING
AND
BING

Yep, "fighting's" the word.

You only use these new plastic protective caps (FSN 5340-880-7666) when you're in action . . . not when your shooter's put up for a day or more. Else condensation'll build up and ruin the bore.

The cap'll keep out rain, dust and dirt, but it won't keep water from seeping into the bore from the chamber end when your rifle gets dunked. This water's got to be removed before you try to fire.

HERE'S WHAT YOU DO! . . . AFTER YOU REMOVE THE CAP.

POINT THE MUZZLE DOWN . . .	CHARGING HANDLE SLIGHTLY REARWARD !	PRESS FORWARD ASSIST TO SEAT ROUND

So get with that routine in para 2-11 to your new -12 TM before you fire off.

MAGAZINE PINUPS!

From 17 to 20's fine, but 21's too many when you're loading cartridges in the magazine of your M16A1 rifle. It won't give you extra fighting power . . . more likely it'll put you out of the fight—'cause that extra round will spread the lips and the ammo won't feed right.

When unloading, never flip the rounds out with another cartridge. You'll spread the lips this way, too. Instead, slide the rounds out straight ahead . . . like they go into the chamber.

INSTEAD
SLIDE
ROUNDS
OUT
STRAIGHT

When you're taking your magazine apart here's as far as you can go. Any further and you might damage it.

1. Stick cartridge point in here to press the floor plate release.
2. Slide out the floor plate.
3. Work the spring back and forth gently as you tug it outward.
4. Stop tugging when the follower reaches the tabs and ears and don't separate the spring from the follower.

Careful . . . you don't stretch or ben the spring and don't bend the tabs. Eas does it all the way.

For cleaning the disassembled ma —Either dunk it in rifle bore clean and shake it good while submerged

OR—scrub the inside with a brus soaked with cleaner

OR—Use a rag soaked in bor cleaner.

Then dry it out good with a swab c rag (or even your shirtail in a pinch

After you clean the inside of th magazine, wipe the spring off and se that it's not busted or deformed. If it OK, apply a very-very-very light coa of lube—using a rag dampened wit LSA.

This mag is coated with dry lubr cant. It doesn't need any lubing excep for the spring.

PUTTING

MAGGIE

TOGETHER

Here's the easy way . . . **gently:**

1. Nose the bullet end of the follower into the body at a 45-degree angle till it touches the inside edge of the body.

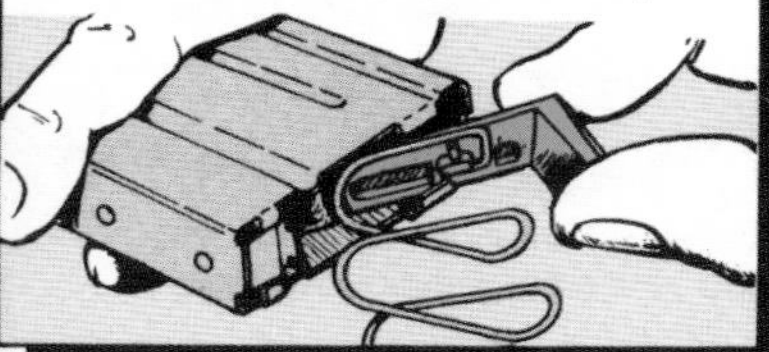

2. Work the other end of the follower into the body.

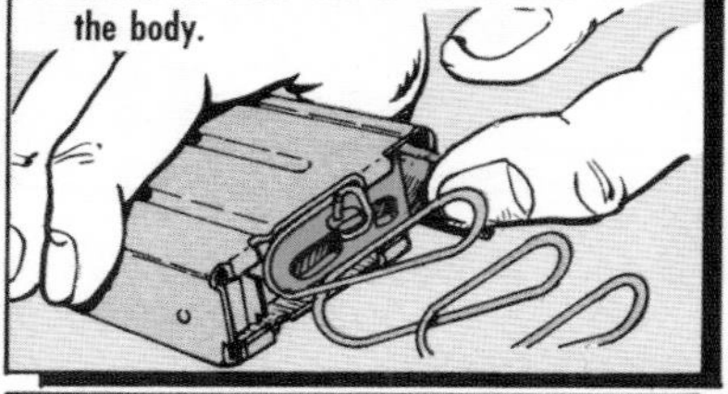

3. Just wiggle the spring into the mag as far as it'll go.

4. Make sure the printing on the floor plate is on the outside. Slide the plate in this way, then press the spring down with your thumb. And make sure the floor plate goes under all 4 tabs, too.

HERE'S AN IMPORTANT **TIP:** IF THE SPRING SHOULD **ACCIDENTALLY** GET SEPARATED FROM THE FOLLOWER, TURN THE MAGAZINE OVER TO YOUR ARMORER! **DON'T** TRY TO FIX IT YOURSELF. LOOKS EASY, SURE, BUT WITHOUT THE RIGHT TOOL YOU'D DAMAGE THE SPRING... AND END UP WITH FEEDING TROUBLE.

27

PROTECTING YOUR MAG

PROTECT ME, YOU BIG STRONG GUY!

Not easy, that's for sure, when you're wading streams and rice paddies or in heavy rainfall. Normally clean water itself is not harmful. Brackish water—that's another story. But the real harm comes when you don't do anything about it after your stuff gets wet.

Here're some ideas that might help:

1 When fording, try to keep your mags out of the water. This means holding your rifle 'way up there and, if you can, keep the pouch with the spares above the water line.

2 Soon as you come out of the drink—if Charlie's not interfering, natch—take the mags out and shake 'em good a couple of times to get rid of most of the water.

3 Then at the first breather—when you're sure Charlie's not around—empty each magazine, wipe it dry inside and out with your shirttail or swab and then clean both the ammo and the magazine.

TIP: You M16A1 zapmen using a plastic bag (FSN 1005-052-6942) to protect your loaded magazine, use your head. The bag's apt to collect condensation if it's wet or humid, so, check your bagged magazine daily. If you see beads of condensation inside the bag, take off the bag and dry it, the magazine and the ammo thoroughly—and don't forget that little film of LSA on the magazine spring. This bag, y'know, won't excuse you from regular PM chores.

F'goshsakes, never put oil of any kind—including LSA—on the cartridge or inside your magazine! Lube ruins ammo and collects gook—could leave you helpless in a fight! This mag is coated with dry lubricant. It doesn't need any lubing except for the spring—and that only very lightly, with LSA.

Take care of your magazines—and hang on to 'em. Sure, there're plenty of 'em in supply—world-wide—but they could get mighty scarce in your own sector. So, protect 'em from dents (aluminum can't take rough treatment) —and especially, remember to bring those "empties" back. The one you save just might save you some day.

ENEMY SUPPLY

VEHICLE RIFLE HOLDERS

No matter what size truck you pilot where the action is -- any where from a 1/4-ton M151 to a 10-ton M123 -- make sure it's equipped with a bracket to hold your (and your side-kick's) M16A1 or M14 rifles.

If you jockey one of those new 1-1/4-ton M715's or M725's, no sweat. They come equipped with a single rifle bracket mounted on the left side of the panel behind the driver's seat.

But, on all other trucks, you install a pair of brackets right up front. The M151 gets one to the left of the driver and the other to the right of the passenger. The others get 2 located just to the right of the driver.

Anyway, the item you want goes by the moniker: KIT, MOUNTING, RIFLE BRACKET, and answers to FSN 2590-045-9611. The bracket will handle either the M16A1 or the M14, though you may have to do a little maneuvering to get the M16 to fit the way you want it.

Here's where to look for installation and parts poop for the various vehicles:
  TB 9-2300-209-20 (6 Feb 67) for 3/4-, 2-1/2-, 5- and 10-ton trucks.
  TM 9-2320-218-20 (Apr 63) with Change 2 (16 Nov 65) for the M151 1/4-tonners.

5.56-MM SUBMACHINE GUN, XM177E2:

So you've got the new XM-77E1 or XM177E2 5.56-MM Submachine Gun —or you're expecting it on the next chopper!

HERE COMES SHORTY!

So, here's the Numbah One poop on it:

It needs exactly the same tender loving care and cleaning as the M16A1 rifle. Give out with this TLC and you'll escape the woes some Joes had because they skimped PM on their Sweet 16's.

Yeah, this Shorty's pretty much like the M16A1—it's just shorter in the barrel and hand guards, has an adjustable butt stock and a combination noise and flash suppressor. Most of its other parts are common to the M16A1.

All cleaning and lubing requirements are the same, too—and if you don't do em Shorty'll act up. Even the cleaning tools are the same.

You'll find all the parts common to the Shorty in POMM 9-1005-294-14.

SAME AS M16A1 — SAME SIGHT — ADJUSTABLE BUTT STOCK — SHORTER HAND GUARD — SPECIAL NOISE AND FLASH SUPPRESSOR

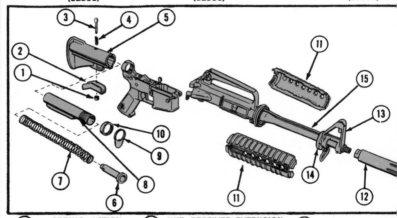

HERE ARE THE PARTS FOR SHORTY-

① NUT, LOCK PIN
FSN 5310-917-1215
(62368)

② LEVER, RELEASE
FSN 1005-914-3224
(62360)

③ PIN, LOCK
FSN 1005-914-3229
(62361)

④ SPRING, LOCKING
FSN 1005-916-9178
(62369)

⑤ STOCK, BUTT, SLI
FSN 1005-914-29
(62359)

⑥ BUFFER ASSEMBL
FSN 1005-914-457
(62382)

⑦ SPRING, ACTION
FSN 1005-914-4564
(62373)

⑧ EXTENSION, LOWER
RECEIVER
FSN 1005-914-2929
(62356)

⑨ PLATE, END
RECEIVER
FSN 1005-914-2942
(62358)

⑩ NUT, RECEIVER EXTENSION
FSN 5310-917-1153
(62357)

⑪ HANDGUARD ASSEMBLY
FSN 1005-914-4572
(62381)

⑫ SUPPRESSOR,
NOISE AND FLASH
FSN 1005-914-3902
(62370)

⑬ BARREL AND
SIGHT ASSEMBLY
FSN 1005-914-456
(62378)

⑭ CAP, HANDGUARI
FSN 1005-914-292
(62346)

⑮ TUBE, GAS ASSEI
FSN 1005-914-3
(62366)

HEADQUARTERS
DEPARTMENT OF THE ARMY
WASHINGTON, D. C., *1 July 1969*

The proponent agency of this pamphlet is the U. S. Army Materiel Command. Users are invited to send comments and suggested improvements on DA Form 2028 (Recommended Changes to Publications) to the Commanding General, U. S. Army Weapons Command, ATTN: AMSWE-SMM, Rock Island, Illinois 61201.

By Order of the Secretary of the Army:

W. C. WESTMORELAND,
General, United States Army,
Chief of Staff.

Official:
  KENNETH G. WICKHAM,
  Major General, United States Army,
  The Adjutant General.

Distribution:
  To be distributed in accordance with DA Form 12-11, requirements for Rifle, 5.56MM, XM16E1.

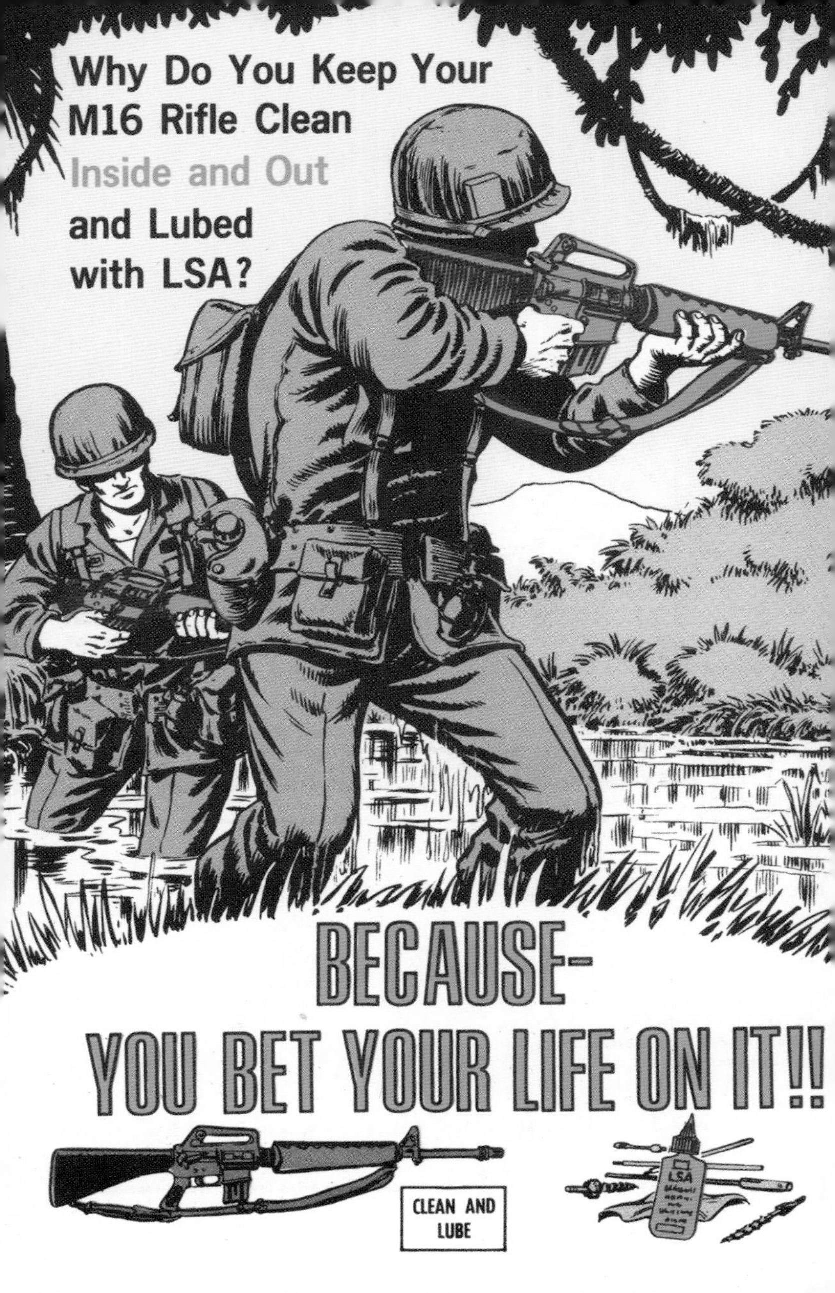
Why Do You Keep Your
M16 Rifle Clean
Inside and Out
and Lubed
with LSA?
BECAUSE-
YOU BET YOUR LIFE ON IT!!
CLEAN AND
LUBE
LSA

A BRIEF ILLUSTRATED HISTORY OF THE AR-15/M16 RIFLE

By Robert A. Sadowski

1955–56 HOLLYWOOD, CA: ArmaLite Corporation, a small machine shop, becomes a subdivision of Fairchild Engine and Airplane Corporation and hires Eugene Stoner as chief design engineer. ArmaLite's business plan is to design small arms to be sold or licensed. Stoner, Robert Fremont, and L. James Sullivan all work on developing new small-arms designs.

FALL 1956: ArmaLite develops the first AR-10 prototype in 7.62mm, and four test rifles are hurriedly submitted into the U.S. Army's tests for a replacement for the M1 Garand. The AR-10 is unlike any rifle in the competition—non-reciprocating charging handle, hinged upper and lower components, select fire, gas-operated direct impingement system, lightweight aluminum receiver, synthetic stock, aluminum/steel barrel, to name just a few unique design characteristics. Springfield Armory submits their T44E4 and Fabrique Nationale submits their FAL. During torture testing, the AR-10's barrel bursts, and the military ultimately opts for Springfield Armory's T44, a more conventional design.

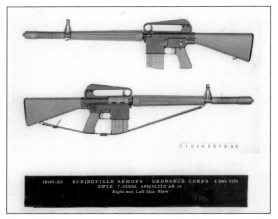

The AR-10 took a very unconventional path in weapons design in the late 1950s. Courtesy of Springfield Armory National Historic Site.

1957: The Army designates Springfield Armory's T44 the M14. ArmaLite licenses the AR-10 to Artillerie Inrichtingen in Holland. Samuel Cummings, an international arms dealer, orders 50 AR-10s. These rifles are built by ArmaLite and become known as the "Hollywood Model." Cummings inks a contract with Nicaragua for 7,500 rifles. Portugal, Sudan, Guatemala, Cuba, Italy, and Burma governments all purchase AR-10s. Army Command begins development of a .22-caliber military rifle as a direct result of the SALVO research project, in which high velocity, .22-caliber weapons were tested and found to have the same lethal power as .30-caliber weapons, without the severe recoil or lack of control in full auto fire and with the added benefit of a soldier being able to carry a greater number of cartridges. ArmaLite develops the AR-15, borrowing many features from the AR-10. It is space-age and high-tech compared to other military rifles at the time.

1958: Ten AR-15 rifles are tested at Fort Banning, with additional tests conducted at the Aberdeen Proving Ground and in the Arctic. The tests discover the design needs some modifications, but final reports state the AR-15 is a viable replacement for the .30-caliber M14.

The M14 was a traditional military rifle design using wood and steel with a piston operating system. Courtesy of Springfield Armory.

1959: After a review of the reports, General Maxwell Taylor orders continued production of the M14 rifle over adopting the AR-15. Fairchild sells manufacturing and marketing rights to Colt's Patent Firearms and Manufacturing Corporation in Hartford, Connecticut. Colt, which now employs Stoner, begins the hard sell of the AR-15.

1960 HAGERSTOWN, MD: Colt demonstrates the AR-15 to General Curtis LeMay, Air Force Chief of Staff, who is convinced of the killing power of the AR-15 and requests an order for 80,000 AR-15 rifles for the Air Force. The military is loath to have two different caliber rifles in service. President John F. Kennedy turns down LeMay's request.

1961 SOUTH VIETNAM: Project AGILE is launched to deter the communist presence in South Vietnam. A handful of AR-15s are sent to South Vietnam for testing. The test rifles are well received by users.

1962 SOUTH VIETNAM: Another shipment of 1,000 AR-15s are sent to South Vietnam where they are used by Special Operations forces and advisors. In combat the rifles prove effective, and the killing power of the 5.56mm cartridge makes devastating kills among the enemy.

1963 WASHINGTON, D.C.: U.S. Secretary of Defense Robert McNamara needs to make a decision. The AGILE test favors adoption of the AR-15 while the military stands behind the M14. Another test is conducted of the M14, AR-15, and AK-47, but the Army report is biased toward the M14. McNamara halts production of the M14 since it won't meet the need of the military. He orders the AR-15 to be adopted and immediately issued, though there are reports of some needed enhancements, like a chrome-lined barrel and a forward assist to help push the bolt closed, in the case that fouling impedes the bolt going into battery. Along with the needed design changes, there are not sufficient quantities of 5.56mm ammo on hand. Two versions of the rifle are made: the M16 without a forward assist for the Air Force and the XM16E1 with a forward assist for the other branches of the military. The Army orders 85,000 XM16E1 rifles and the Air Force 19,000 M16s.

The first M16 with triangular handguard and without a forward assist. Courtesy of Springfield Armory National Historic Site.

1964 WASHINGTON, D.C.: The .223 Remington/ 5.56x45mm cartridge is officially adopted by the U.S. Army for use in the AR-15 platform. Technically, the .223 Remington and the 5.56x45mm are slightly different, with 5.56 brass cases heavier than commercial .223 cases. Chambers and throats are also slightly different.

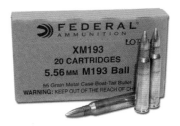

The gelatin block shows the effect of a 5.56mm caliber 75-grain Boat Tail Hollow Point bullet. Courtesy of Hornady.

1965 VIETNAM: The XM16E1 is issued to troops without cleaning supplies or instructions. A short-barreled variant, the XM177 Commando, is also distributed. The gas impingement system was designed as self-cleaning and requiring minimal maintenance. While in combat, soldiers begin to experience stoppages. Cartridge cases are lodged in the chamber after the bullet is fired. U.S. soldiers are found killed, with their rifles disassembled beside them as they tried to fix their weapons. Documented evidence builds, and a Congressional investigation ensues. The main problem for the failure-to-extract stoppages is discovered in the gun powder of the ammunition. The nitrocellulose-based powder the rifle was designed to use was replaced with a nitrocellulose and nitroglycerin-based powder that leaves a residue in the rifle's mechanism.

A typical grunt in 'Nam toting an M16. Courtesy of Springfield Armory National Historic Site.

1967: The deficiencies in the XM16E1 are addressed, and the rifle is standardized as the M16A1 with a chrome-lined chamber, a recoil buffer modified for the ammo, triangular handguard, and duck-bill flash suppressor. A cleaning kit is supplied to troops, too. Will Eisner's comic manual is also passed out to G.I.s. With the design changes and maintenance training, the reliability of the rifle increases, and it gains acceptance and approval with the troops.

1970s: Numerous countries opt for the M16-style rifle, and to this day it is used by fifteen NATO nations.

Originally the M16 was not issued with a cleaning kit, but that soon changed after it jammed in combat. Courtesy of Springfield Armory National Historic Site.

1973: The Civilian Marksmanship Program authorizes the use of the AR-15 rifle in the Service Rifle category for National Matches and defines the AR-15 as "Rifle, Caliber 5.56mm, M16, or commercial equivalent, and service cartridge."

Courtesy of Civilian Marksmanship Program.

The M16 overshadows other rifles in service rifle competition.

MID 1980s: The Marines ask for design changes, and the M16A2 is extensively enhanced, with a thicker barrel with new twist-rate, new sights, different flash suppressor, brass deflector, and three-round burst, among other modifications. The M16A3 is a fully auto version for use by SEAL forces.

1982 COLORADO SPRINGS, CO: Olympia Arms begins to manufacture ARs and is the first company to produce flat-top upper receivers, free floating aluminum hand guards, pistol caliber conversions, and AR-15-based pistols.

1983 HARTFORD, CT: Colt's patents expire and several manufacturers start manufacturing AR-15 rifles.

1986: After the FBI Miami shootout and the Norco shootout in Norco, California, in 1980, U.S. law enforcement agencies begin to equip themselves with ARs.

1990s: AR popularity surges with varmint hunters as manufacturers like Rock River Arms, DPMS, Ambush Firearms (Daniel Defense), LaRue Tactical, and others create extremely accurate coyote rifles.

The AR-15 is law enforcement's go-to rifle. Courtesy of Colt Defense.

1993 St. Cloud, MN: DPMS Firearms introduces their AR-15 Series of rifles. Formerly Defense Procurement Manufacturing Services, DPMS has been in AR parts manufacturing since 1986.

1994 Washington, D.C.: The term "assault weapon" becomes a political and legal flash point and is used to describe several civilian semi-automatic variants of military full-automatic rifles. A ban is put in place by President Bill Clinton that defines an assault weapon as a semi-automatic firearm with the ability to accept a detachable magazine and at least two or more of the following characteristics: folding stock, pistol grip, bayonet mount, flash suppressor, and grenade launcher. The M4 carbine and M4A1 variants are adopted by the U.S. Military. Both are shorter and lighter than the M16A2 and are designed for close-quarter combat. The M4A1 is fully automatic and intended for Special Ops forces.

1995: The U. S. Army Team wins the National Trophy Team Match with M16s, creating a massive switch of competitors from M14s to M16/ARs. As competitors begin using longer bullets in the 5.56mm cartridge, M16/AR rifles become competitive at 600 yards.

The M4 equipped with optics became common in early 21st-century conflicts. Courtesy of Colt Defense.

1998 Lake Havasu City, AZ: Professional Ordnance introduces an AR-15 with a carbon-fiber lower called the Carbon 15.

2001 Afghanistan: The Marines order officers to carry the M4 in lieu of the M9 handgun.

This soldier in Afghanistan has a rifle equipped with a 40mm grenade launcher. Courtesy of United States Army.

2003 Windham, ME/Iraq: Bushmaster purchases Professional Ordnance and offers AR-15s with carbon lowers and traditional forged aluminum lowers. The war in Iraq begins and M4s show their worth in city fighting.

2004 WASHINGTON, D.C.: Under President George W. Bush's administration, the assault rifle ban is allowed to expire. Many states still require post-ban configurations: welded muzzle brake, no bayonet lug, fixed buttstock, and 10-round magazines. The commercial market for "black rifles" increases dramatically.

MID 2000S: Manufacturers offer ARs in different calibers—6.8 SPC, 6.5 Grendel, .308, .450 Bushmaster, .50 Beowolf, .30 RAR, to name just a few—and big game hunters discover the AR-15 and AR-10 platforms make excellent hunting rifles. Like former military rifles of yore, ARs are seen in hunting camps.

Courtesy of National Sport Shooting Foundation.

ARs are the firearms of choice for many hunters today.

2006 SOUTHPORT, CT: Ruger announces the SR-556, an AR that uses a piston-driven system in lieu of gas impingement. Though Ruger was not the first manufacturer to produce a piston-operated AR, they continue the piston vs. gas operating system debate.

An example of Ruger's SR-556 piston system. Many feel a piston system is better than the gas impingement system. Courtesy of Ruger.

2007 NEW BRITAIN, CT: Stag Arms introduces a left-handed AR.

Stag Arms left-handed AR-15. Courtesy of Stag Arms.

2008 MADISON, NC/WASHINGTON, D.C./THE HEARTLAND, U.S.A.: Remington introduces the R-15, a camo-finished varmint-hunting rifle built by Bushmaster. Cerberus Capital owns Remington, Bushmaster, DPMS, and numerous other firearm manufacturers. The next year, Remington offers the R-25 in larger calibers like .308, .243, and 7mm-08. The fourth generation M16 is adopted by the U.S. Military as the M16A4, equipped with a removable carry handle and quad Picatinny rail. Pandemics and zombie outbreaks begin with fun competitive shooting events. Zombie Industries targets even bleed dead zombie blood.

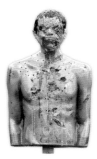

The apocalypse is upon us, and zombie shooting competitors gear up to play their part. Courtesy of Zombie Industries and Brownells (center image).

2009: U.S. Military proposes changes to the M4, including an electronic round counter, heavier barrel, and possible replacement of direct gas impingement system with a gas-piston system.

2010 WASHINGTON, D.C.: Some 37,000 M4A1s are contracted by the U.S. Army from Colt to be filled by 2011.

2012 HARTFORD, CT: Colt introduces the LE901 modular AR platform that converts from a 7.62mm/.308-caliber upper to a 5.56mm/.223 upper. It also uses Colt's monolithic upper design that allows the barrel to free float.

2013-2014 MADISON, NC: Remington Arms Company will be the first manufacturer other than Colt to provide the military with M4A1s. Some 24,000 are contracted.

Colt's LE901 is designed to take a 7.62mm/.308-caliber upper as well as a 5.56mm/.223 upper. Courtesy of Colt Defense.

Shooter's Bible Guide to Firearms Assembly, Disassembly, and Cleaning

by Robert A. Sadowski

Shooter's Bible, the most trusted source on firearms, is here to bring you a new guide with expert knowledge and advice on gun care. Double-page spreads filled with photos and illustrations provide manufacturer specifications on each featured model and guide you through disassembly and assembly for rifles, shotguns, handguns, and muzzleloaders. Step-by-step instructions for cleaning help you to care for your firearms safely. Never have a doubt about proper gun maintenance when you own *Shooter's Bible Guide to Firearms Assembly, Disassembly, and Cleaning*, a great companion to the original *Shooter's Bible*.

Along with assembly, disassembly, and cleaning instructions, each featured firearm is accompanied by a brief description and list of important specs, including manufacturer, model, similar models, action, calibers/gauge, capacity, overall length, and weight. With these helpful gun maintenance tips, up-to-date specifications, detailed exploded view line drawings, and multiple photographs for each firearm, *Shooter's Bible Guide to Firearms Assembly, Disassembly, and Cleaning* is a great resource for all firearm owners.

$19.95 Paperback

ALSO AVAILABLE

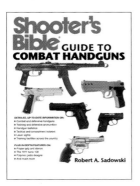

"Ultimately, anyone who owns or plans to purchase a handgun for self-defense will benefit from this superlative guide."

—*Shooting Illustrated*

Shooter's Bible Guide to Combat Handguns

by Robert A. Sadowski

For more than 100 years, *Shooter's Bible* has been the ultimate comprehensive resource for shooting enthusiasts across the board. Trusted by everyone from competitive shooters and hunters to those who keep firearms for protection, this leading series is always expanding. Here is the first edition of *Shooter's Bible Guide to Combat Handguns*—your all-encompassing resource with up-to-date information on combat and defensive handguns, training and defensive ammunition, handgun ballistics, tactical and concealment holsters, accessories, training facilities, and more. No *Shooter's Bible* guidebook is complete without a detailed products section showcasing handguns from all across the market.

Author Robert Sadowski proves to be a masterful instructor on all aspects of handguns, providing useful information for every reader, from those with combat handgun experience in military and law enforcement fields to private citizens, first-timers, and beyond.

$19.95 Paperback